Mom

Erin

Dad

One Million Trees

A True Story

Wonder Dog

Me

Shannon

Kristen Balouch

MARGARET FERGUSON BOOKS
HOLIDAY HOUSE · NEW YORK

One day after school, Mom handed me and my sisters suitcases, and Dad handed us packing lists.

*I loved my math class and knew I would miss it.

What I packed.

We left our
little red house
in California and
flew to Canada, where
we switched to a seaplane.
Then we flew over mountains,
between mountains, and
around mountains,
before landing on the water
next to a little town
on Vancouver Island.

Mountains!

Pwetty!

Amazing!

*Bonjour, mes amis.

She said *Hello, my friends* in French.

What did she say?

FIRE DEPARTMENT

We motored to a dock where a crew of 24 Canadians who mostly spoke French met us with trailers, campers, and trucks.

Rosemary

Claude Simon Pierre Aimée Dr. Cello Byron Martha Elvie Vince Gee

*Bonjour, mes amis (pronounced bawn-zhoor mays ah-mee) = Hello, my friends

Inside the trucks were boxes, and inside the boxes were . . .

Alex

Ted

Sprout

Daniel   Tobi   Anderson   Teri   Pat   Lee   Bouchard   Edmund   Paula   Wayne

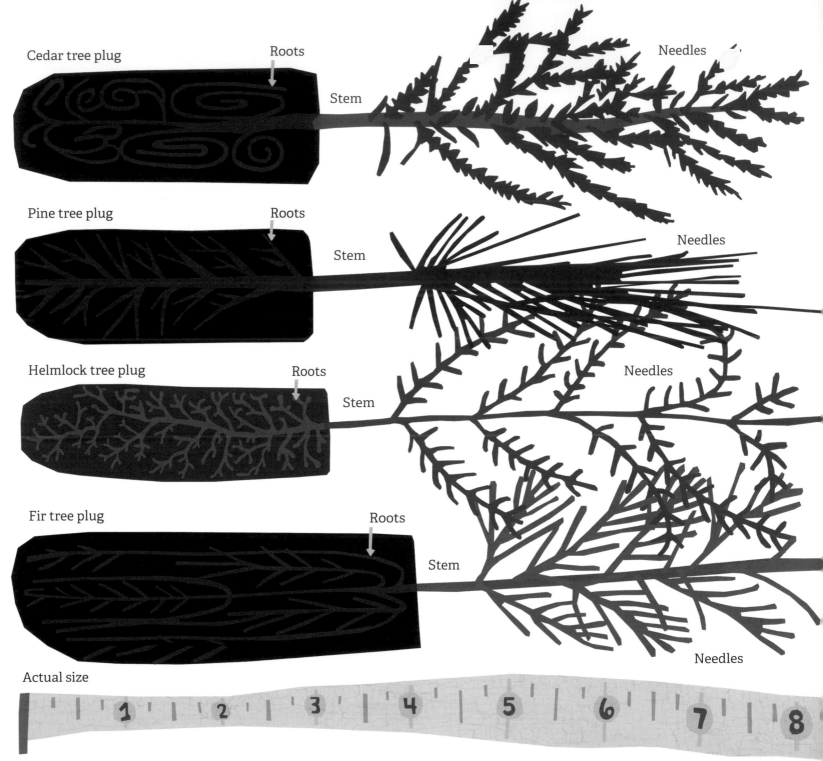

Cedar tree plug — Roots — Stem — Needles

Pine tree plug — Roots — Stem — Needles

Helmlock tree plug — Roots — Stem — Needles

Fir tree plug — Roots — Stem — Needles

Actual size

1 2 3 4 5 6 7 8

Baby trees raised in trays are called plugs by horticulturists, people who are expert gardeners.

TREES!
One MILLION of them!

Each truck had 500 boxes of trees.

Each box had 500 baby trees.

How many trees were in 1 truck?
500 x 500 = ?*

How many trucks did it take to hold 1 million trees?
1,000,000 ÷ number of trees in a truck = ?**

9 | | 10 | | 11 | | 12 | |

*250,000 trees in each truck   ** 1,000,000 ÷ 250,000 = 4 trucks

Pacific Ocean

I wonder how you say *fish in French?

We drove along a narrow, curvy, bumpy road until we came to a river, where we set up camp.

Woof!

Our tent

Cook shack

*Fish = poisson (pronounced pwa-sawn)

Mad Dog

Mothership

One of the tree trucks

The crew even brought a bathtub.

Candy stash

Dad set up our tent.

*Tree = arbre (pronounced are-bruh)

The cook shack was a truck outfitted with a stove, refrigerator, and sink!

The cooking pots were so big that my sister Erin could hide in them.

Mom organized the cook shack. She was going to be the camp cook.

*Merci (pronounced mehr-see) = Thank you

The next morning everyone ate breakfast,

then grabbed their lunches and tools.

My sisters and Wonder Dog stayed with Mom,

but I went with Dad. I wanted to help him plant trees.

Camp

Dad drove one of the trucks to the planting site.

The road hadn't been used for a long time.

There were some obstacles.

Fallen trees

Mothership was our home-base bus at the planting site.

*Bear

*Bear = ours (pronounced oors)

*Moose

Baby moose are cute, but don't get too close.

*Whale

Waterfall

Breakdown

Logging trucks shared the narrow roads with us. They were big and scary.

Broken bridge

Sometimes logs fell off the trucks.

Treacherous road

Mud pit

Mad Dog was our most dependable truck. It had lost its hood, but it still never, ever broke down.

*Elk

The bush bumper on the front of Mad Dog cleared the road of small bushes.

*Moose = élan (pronunced ae-lawn)   *Whale = baleine (pronunced bah-len)   *Elk = wapiti (pronunced wa-pee-tee)

When we finally made it to the site, there were tree stumps everywhere.

It felt empty and lifeless.

Box of trees

Dad and I got our first box of trees from the truck and he showed me how to plant them.

1. DIG

Depending on the species, choose a spot to plant the tree:

on a mound
(water drains away
and the soil stays drier)

in a depression
(water collects and
keeps the soil moist)

near a stump
(protects a baby tree
from harsh weather)

in a rotted tree
(feeds a baby tree with
rich organic material)

under a bush
(protects a baby tree
from harsh sun)

We planted trees in rows, and once we got to the end of a row, we turned around and planted a new line
of trees back toward the truck. Each person (my dad and I counted as one person) planted two boxes a day.

2. WEDGE
Make a V-shaped opening in the soil with a shovel.

3. TUCK
Tuck the tree in along the back side of the shovel.

4. PAT
Use the toe or side of your boot to fill in the dirt around the tree.

Once we were done, checkers came by and tugged on the trees.

If the tree came out too easily, it needed to be replanted.

If the tree was planted too deep, it needed to be replanted.

If the tree wasn't planted deep enough, it needed to be replanted.

Just right!

The tree plugs had to be snug to the pull and spaced ten feet apart, with the first set of needles 1 inch above the soil level.

Most days I helped Dad. But some days I did my schoolwork and explored or swam with my sisters and Wonder Dog.

Old trees sometimes fall on the ground in the woods and baby trees grow out of them.

Mom says
the number of tree rings
tells how old the tree is.
450 rings mean this
tree is 450 years old.

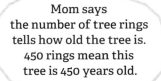

*Wider rings mean conditions
were good and nutrients were
plentiful for the tree that year.*

*Turtle

*Turtle = tortue (pronounced tor-too)

And some days I helped Mom by making dessert for the crew.

Planting trees made everyone hungry, and Mom had to make a lot of food.

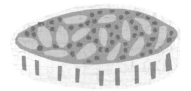

I made 4 apple crumbles.
Each crumble needed 6 apples.

How many apples did I use?
6 + 6 + 6 + 6 = ? or 4 x 6 = ?*

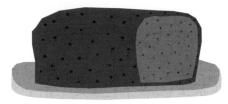

I made 3 loaves of banana bread.
Each loaf needed 4 bananas.

How many bananas did I use?
4 + 4 + 4 = ? or 3 x 4 = ?*

Some Desserts I Made

I made 2 chocolate cakes.
Each cake used 4 eggs.

How many eggs did I use?
4 + 4 = ? or 2 x 4 =?*

I made 2 lemon cakes.
Each cake needed 6 lemons.

How many lemons did I use?
6 + 6 = ? or 2 x 6 = ?*

I made 4 batches of rice pudding.
Each batch needed 1 cup of rice.

How many cups of rice did I use?
1 + 1 + 1 + 1 = ? or 1 x 4 = ?*

I made 4 rhubarb pies.
Each pie needed 8 stalks of rhubarb.

How many stalks did I use?
8 + 8 + 8 + 8 = ? or 4 x 8 = ?*

*Apples = 24   *Bananas = 12   *Eggs = 8   *Lemons = 12   *Cups of rice = 4   *Stalks of rhubarb = 32

*C'est bon (pronounced say bawn) = It's good   *Fox = renard (pronounced ruh-nar)

After 40 days of planting, the tree boxes were empty. The food was gone. Everyone was covered in mud, scratches, and bug bites. But we all went to sleep happy because...

25 planters each planted 1,000 trees a day.
25 x 1,000=25,000.
We planted 25,000 trees for 40 days.
25,000 x 40 = 1,000,000 trees.

*Fini!

*Youpi!

We did it! We planted one million trees!

*Fini (pronounced fee-nee) = Finished *Youpi (pronounced you-pee) = Yay *Hourra (pronounced hoo-rah) = Yippee

We said goodbye to the trees,

swam one more time in the river, and broke down camp.

We flew home to our little red house in California.

*Au revoir!
That's how you say *goodbye* in French.
Au revoir, mes amis.
Au revoir, poisson.
Au revoir, arbre.
Au revoir, baleine.
Au revoir, élan.
Au revoir, ours.
Au revoir, wapiti.
Au revoir, tortue.
Au revoir, renard.

Bye-bye!

Woof!

*Au revoir (pronounced oh ruh-vwar) = Goodbye

Forty years passed.

And today when my children return home from college,

I hand them suitcases. There is something I want us to see.

ONE MILLION TREES!

Author's Note

I grew up among the redwoods of Northern California. One day in 1979, when I was ten years old, my parents decided to take me, my sisters, and our dog, Wonder Dog, tree planting for a season in British Columbia in Canada. We worked on several sites, but I focused *One Million Trees* on the site on Vancouver Island. I did take some liberties in the depiction of animals in the art—moose, caribou, and foxes only live in the interior of British Columbia.

Our job was to plant baby trees that had been grown by the Canadian Forest Service in remote areas where stands of trees had been cut down by the logging industry. A small tree plug was planted for every tree cut by loggers to fulfill the Canadian government's plan for sustainability. Trees planted this way are meant to be cut down again when they reach maturity (about 40–50 years after they've been planted) so there will always be wood to make homes and buildings, furniture, light posts, toys, paper, toothpicks, books, and many more things. These stands of planted trees essentially make "tree farms," not a forest.

All trees help keep our planet healthy. But older forests, known as "old-growth forests," where trees have lived untouched for hundreds of years, are especially important to our environment. They make our air quality exponentially better, absorb more water than younger forests so there is less chance of floods, are the habitat for a diverse variety of species of plants and animals, provide key ingredients for some of our medicines, and keep the soil full of nutrients, as well as stop erosion. They also serve as huge carbon stores for our planet, so cutting them down releases heat-generating compounds into the atmosphere, exasperating our current climate problems. Scientists are still learning the essential roles that trees play in our ecosystems. Sadly, most forests and old-growth forests are still being logged without consideration of the broader impact on the environment.

Tree planting with my family taught me that trees are precious and that old-growth forest trees are irreplaceable. As a child, I saw the amazing things that a small group of people can accomplish when they work together. I am hopeful that if we all join forces and work together, we can make our planet healthy again.

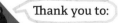 Thank you to:

Margaret Ferguson   Mom   Dad   Shannon Stolfo   Erin Stolfo   Wonder Dog   Bailey Balouch